Time t

M000074172

Andrea Almada
Illustrated by Ann Iosa

Rigby®

A Harcourt Achieve Imprint

www.Rigby.com
1-800-531-5015

"It is time to go," said Papa Duck.

2

"I am too cold,"
said Baby Duck.
She put on a hat.

"I am still too cold," said Baby Duck. She put on a scarf.

"I am still too cold,"
said Baby Duck.
She put on a sock.

8

"I am still too cold,"
said Baby Duck.
She put on a coat.

11

"I am still too cold,"
said Baby Duck.
She put on her boots.

13

"I am still too cold!"
said Baby Duck.

"You will get warm,"
said Papa Duck.

"We will fly away,"
said Mama Duck.
"Then you will
be warm!"